CW01269517

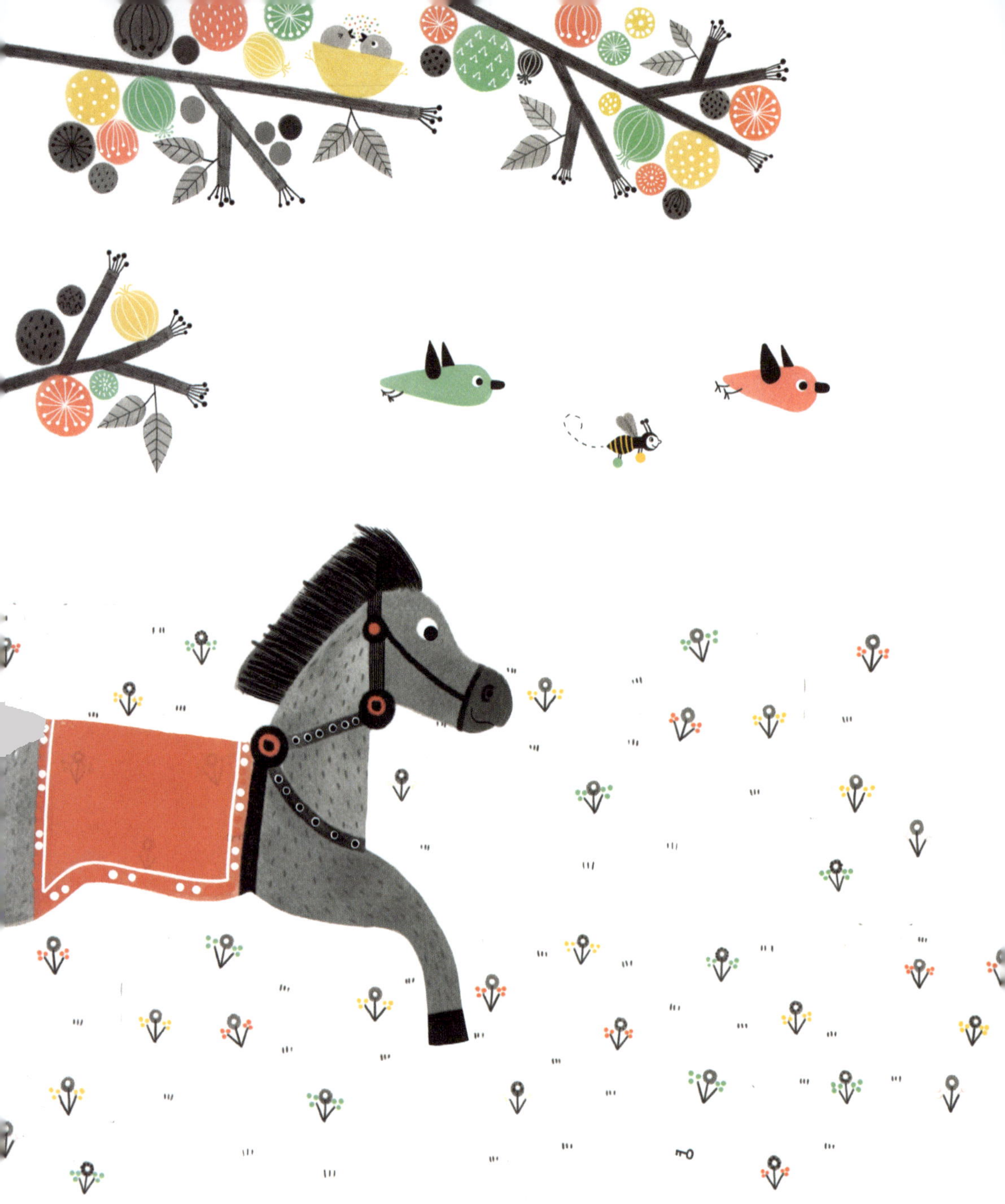

For you, Lillibet, and the wonderful little girl you were.

WSkids
WHITE STAR KIDS

Every day at teatime, Elizabeth meets up with her friends and tells them her story, which starts like this...

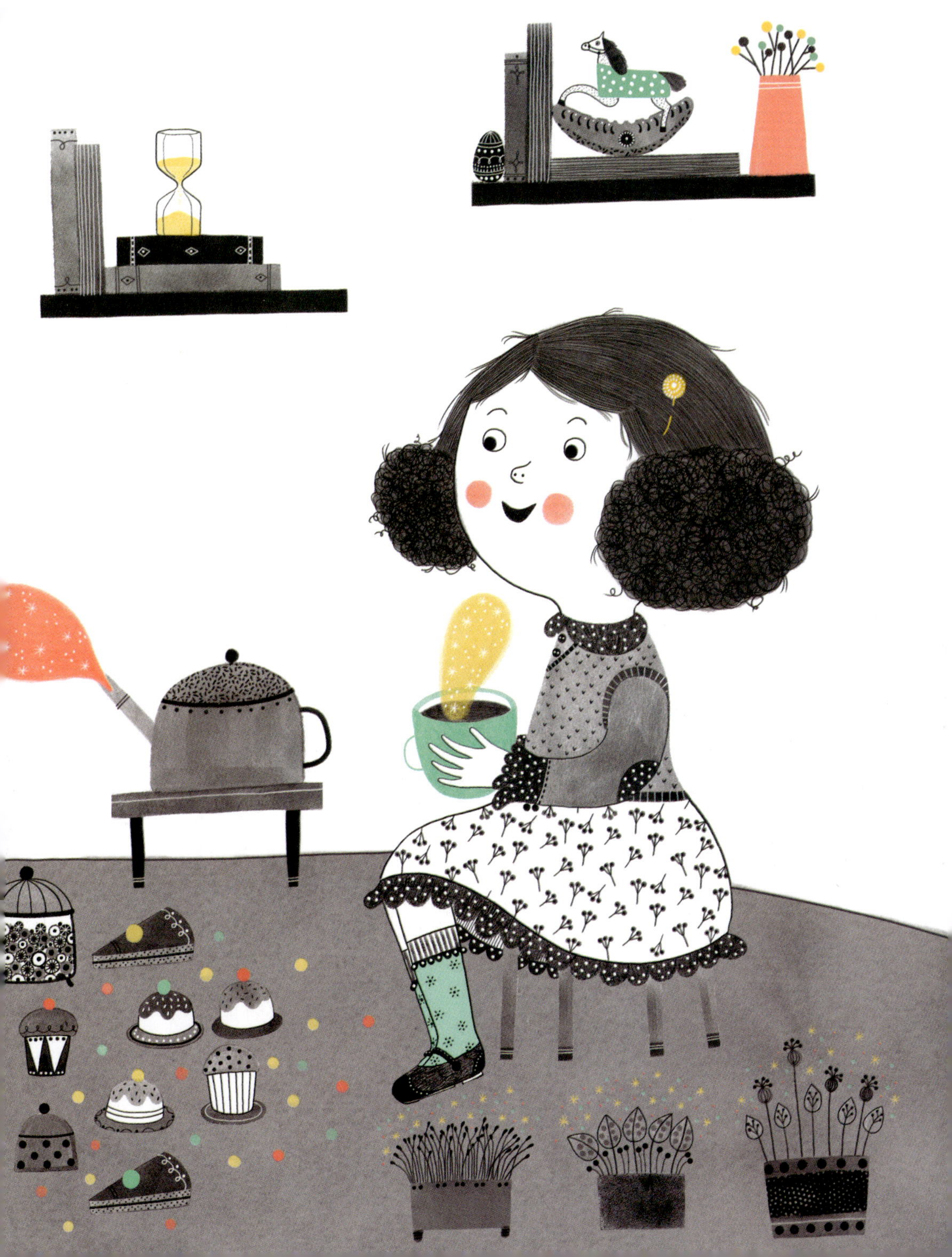

My name is Elizabeth.

My family calls me Lillibet, though,
and I have to say, I really like my nickname!

I live in a beautiful castle in London, surrounded by an enormous park, with my mom, my dad, and my sister, Margaret.

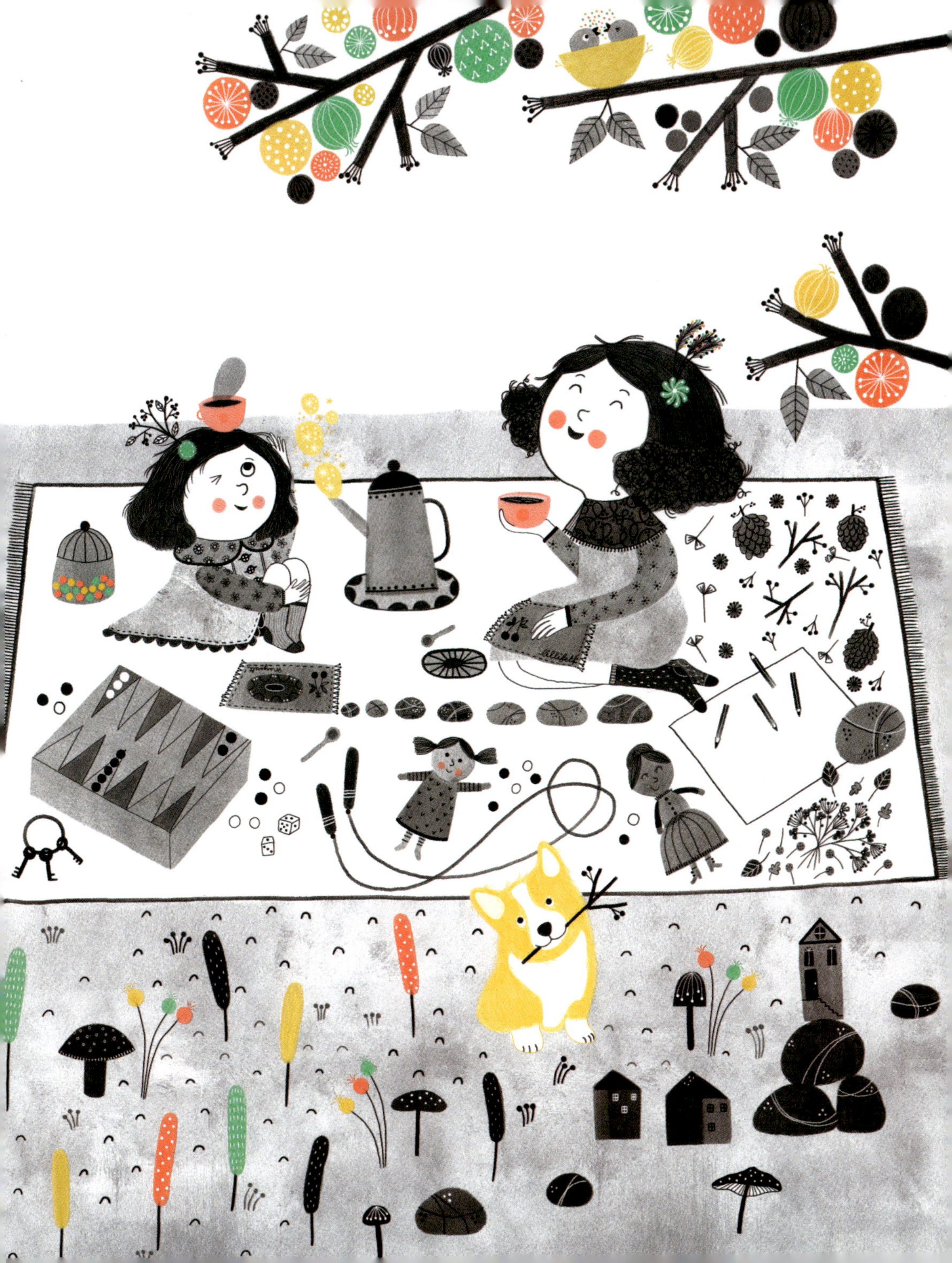

Every day is basically the same.
In the morning I meet with my parents

before dedicating myself to my studies of geography, math, and music.

I have lunch with my family and then take a nap.
In the afternoon I go for a walk and play outside,

take tea with my animal friends, and meet with my parents again for dinner.

In the evening I have my bath and then go to bed, falling asleep to stories of Winnie the Pooh read by my favorite uncle, Uncle David.

Winnie......

During the day I spend a lot of time with my sister, Margaret. If you don't know us, you would be forgiven for mixing us up as we are always dressed the same: velvet jacket, dark skirt, white socks, and patent leather shoes.

Our skirts are always on the move, so mom decided to have drape weights sewn into the hems to weigh them down...clever mom!

lillibet

But the truth is, those who know us well know that my sister Margaret and I are very different. I am precise and tidy—a little too much at times perhaps...

For example, I love putting sugar cubes
in order from the smallest to the largest,
and I cannot go to sleep if my thirty toy horses
aren't lined up perfectly!

I love my house, especially the large park. That's where Peggy – one of my best friends – lives, she's the pony I love riding, even bareback! And then, there are my other friends: my dogs!

Whenever the seamstress adjusts one of my dresses, I take a magnet to the floor searching for all the fallen pins: I certainly don't want my dogs pricking and hurting themselves!

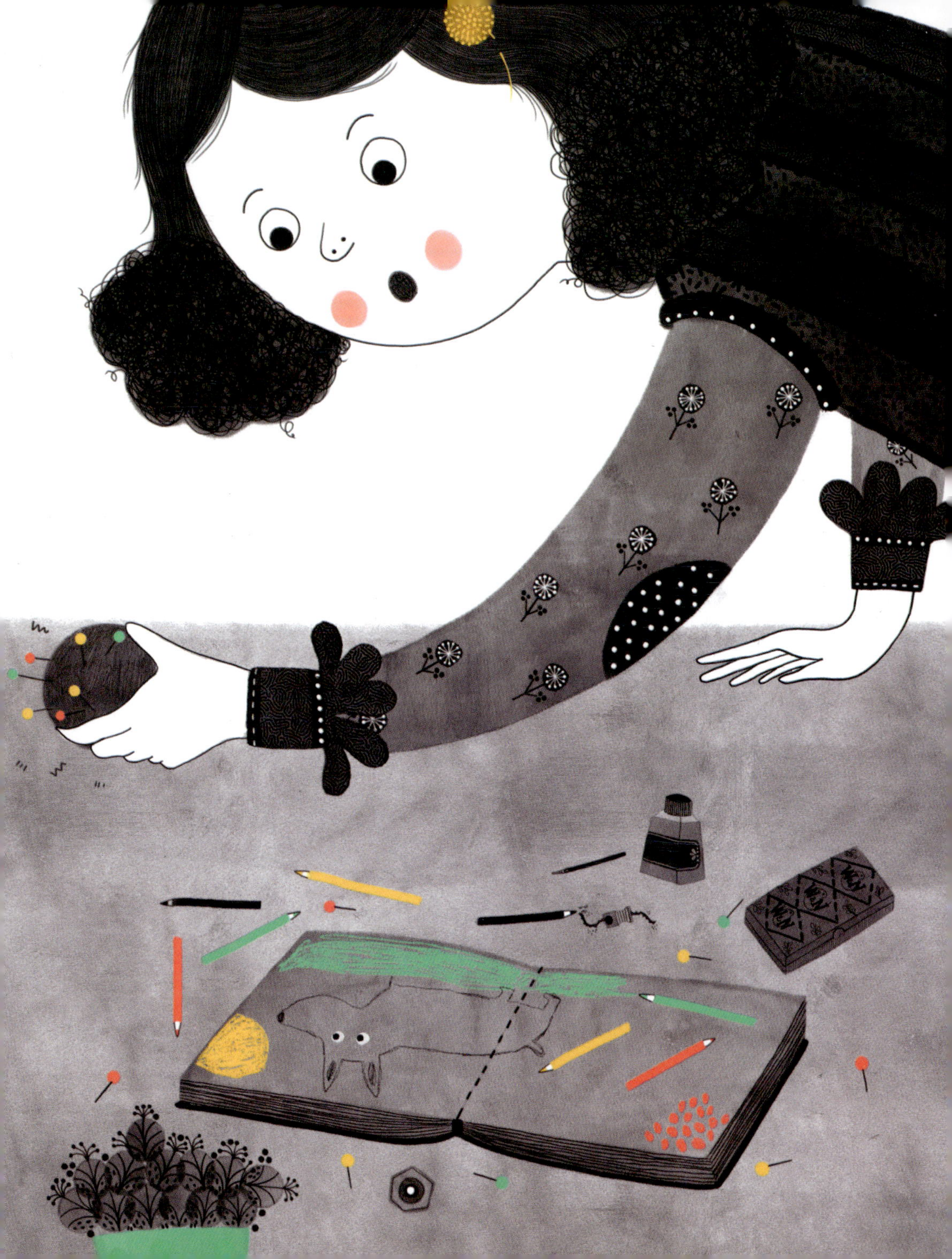

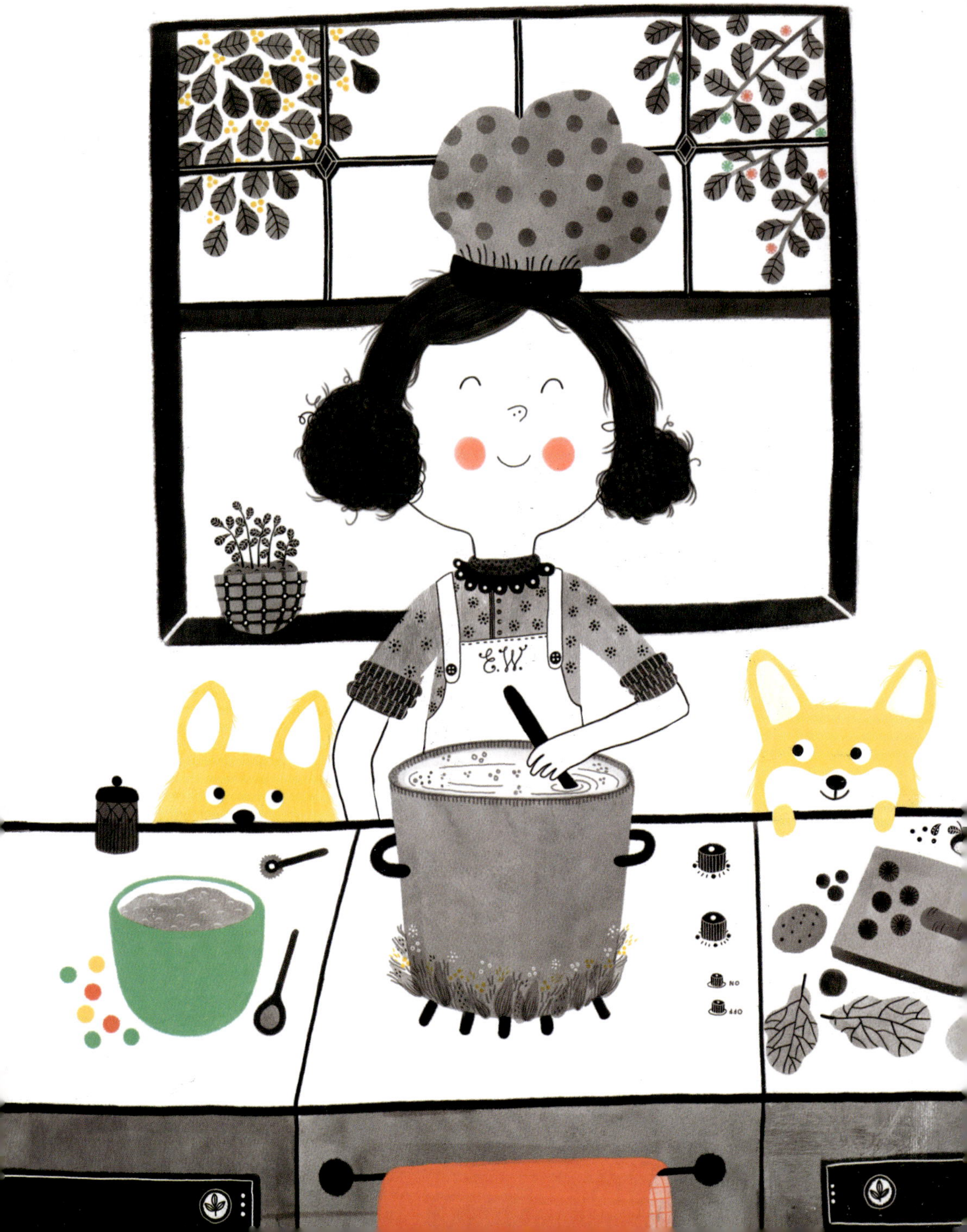
E.W.

For my dogs' dinner, I cook beef fillets and chicken breast covered in gravy, our English sauce that I make myself.

I think they like my gravy, as they won't start to eat until I add it!

In the little free time I have, I like to garden in my white gloves and play in my mini cottage, "The little house," which was a wonderful birthday gift.

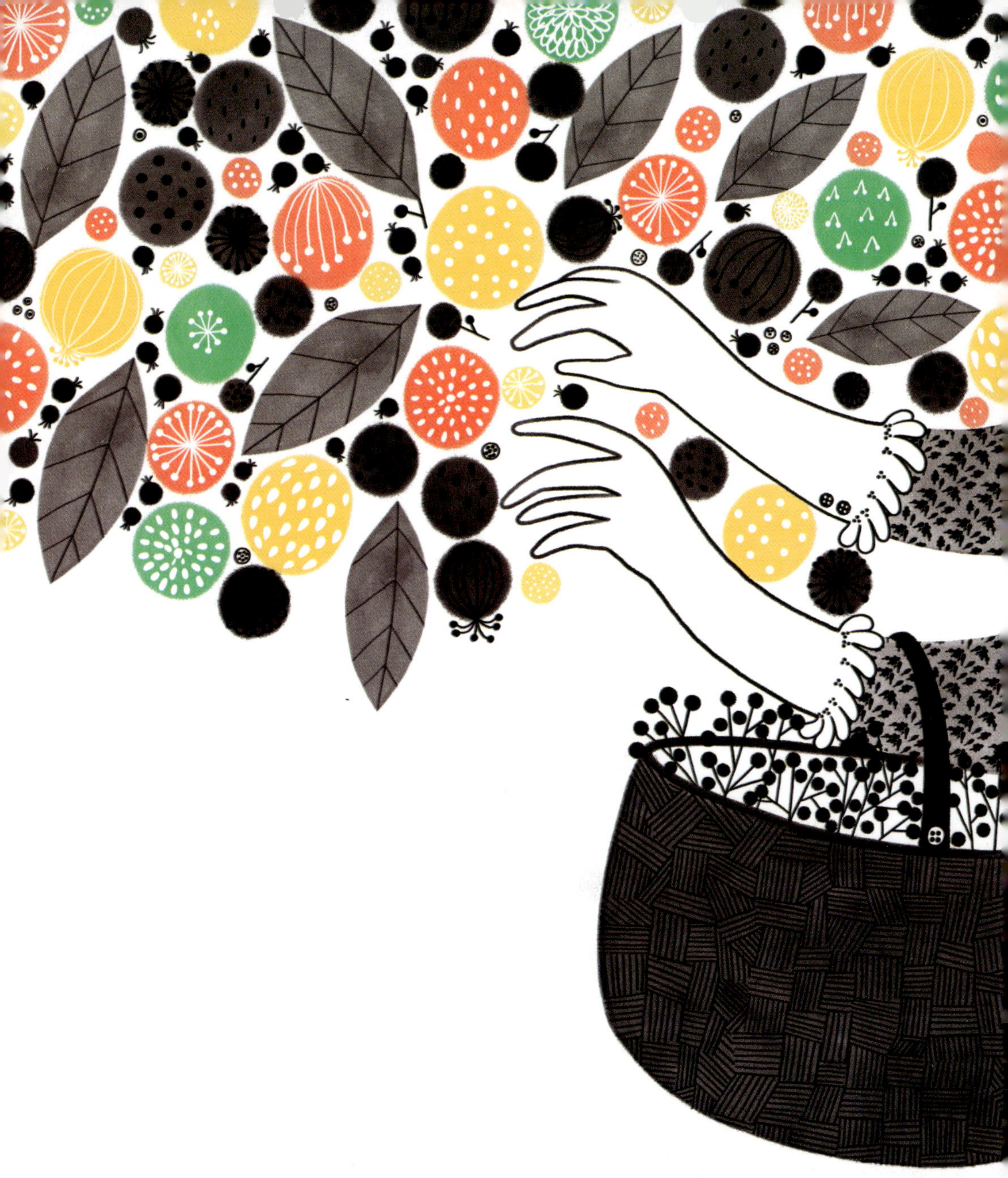

My cottage has a thatched roof, and the windows are blue (my favorite color). There are four bedrooms, a kitchen, and a bookshelf with the complete works of Beatrix Potter.

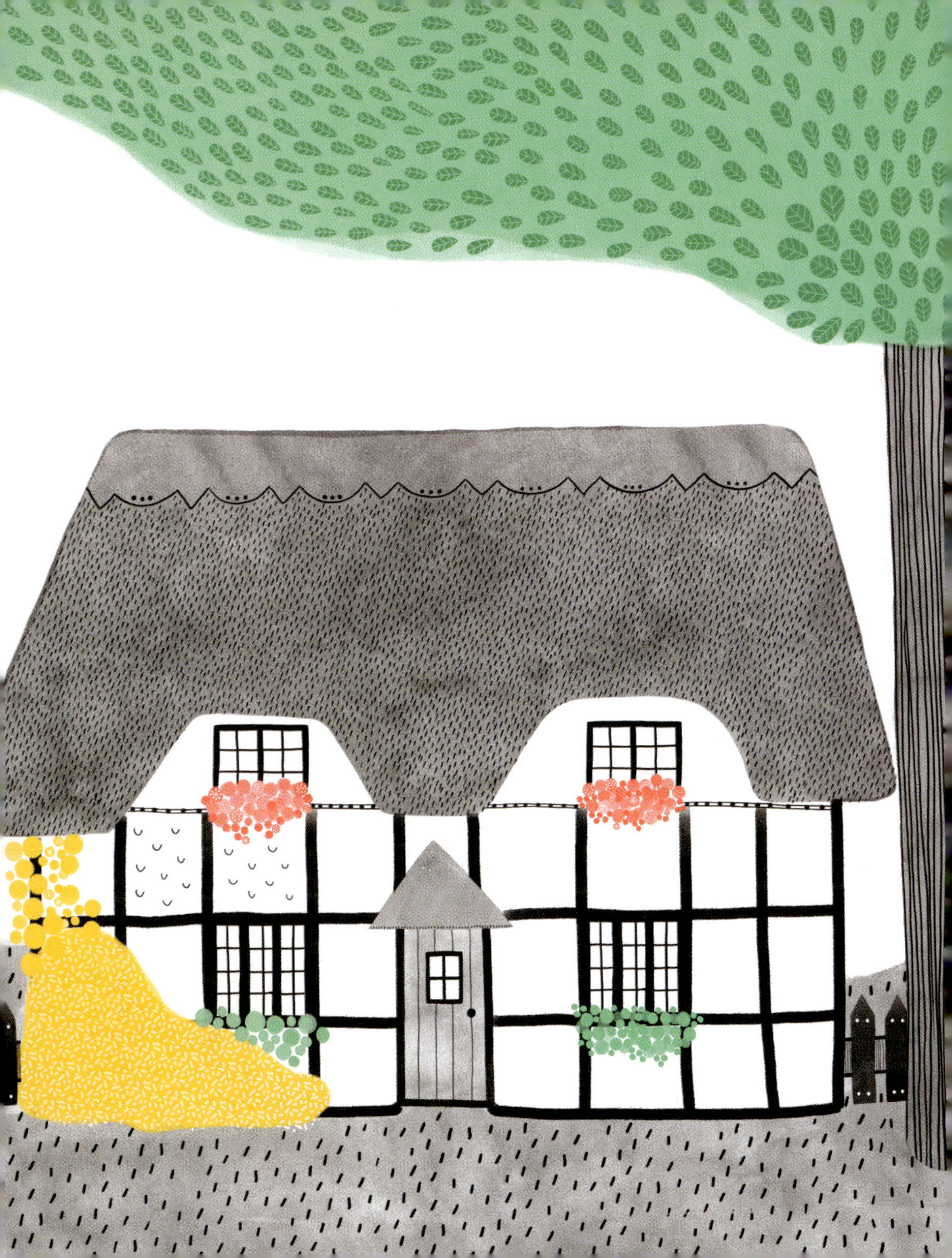

It is here that I organize my tea parties, serving tea to all my friends.

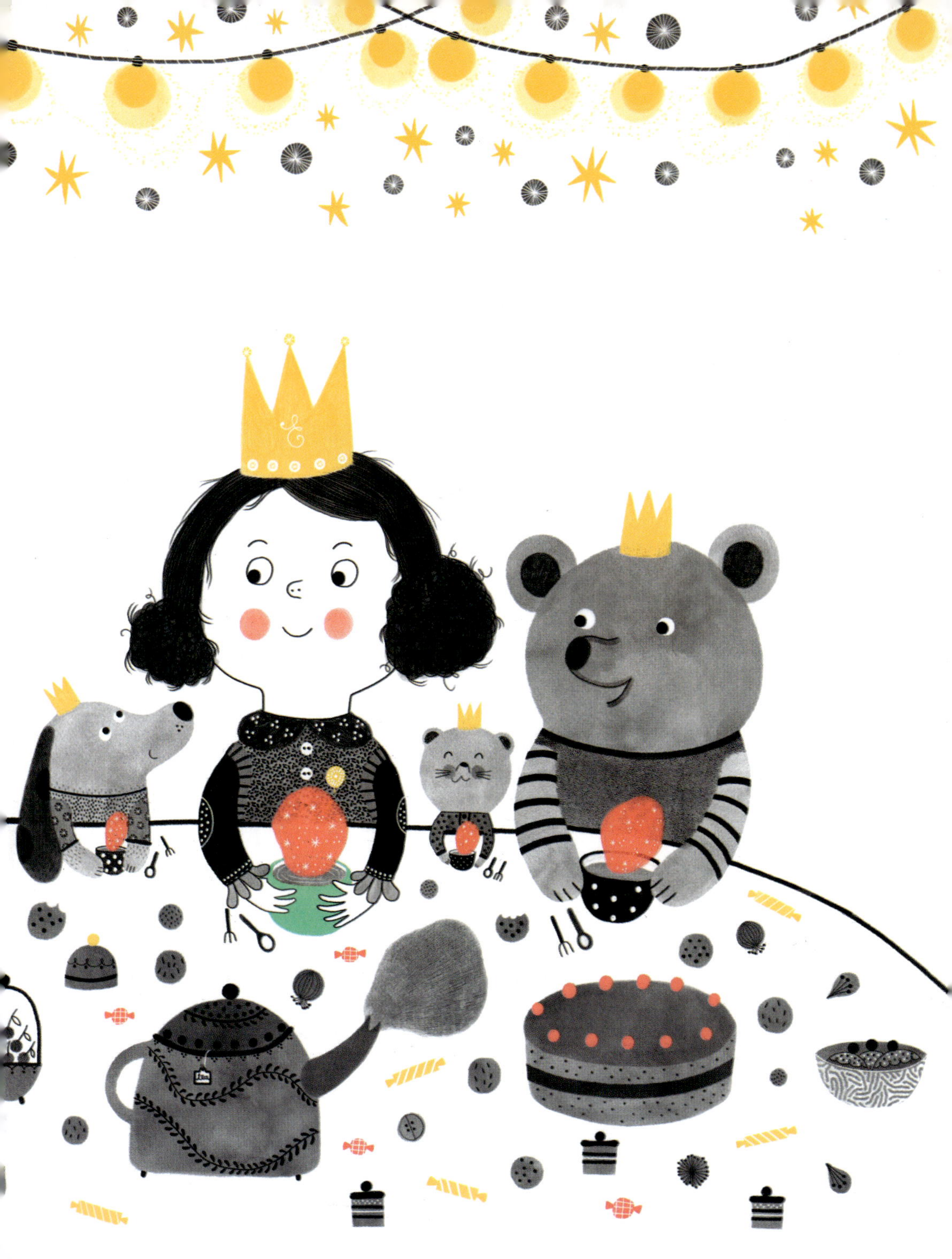

Sometimes I receive some very unusual presents, such as two sloths from Brazil, a small elephant named Jumbo from Cameroon, a crystal model of a corgi dog (my favorite breed of dog), a hockey shirt from Canada, and a pair of cowboy boots from the United States.

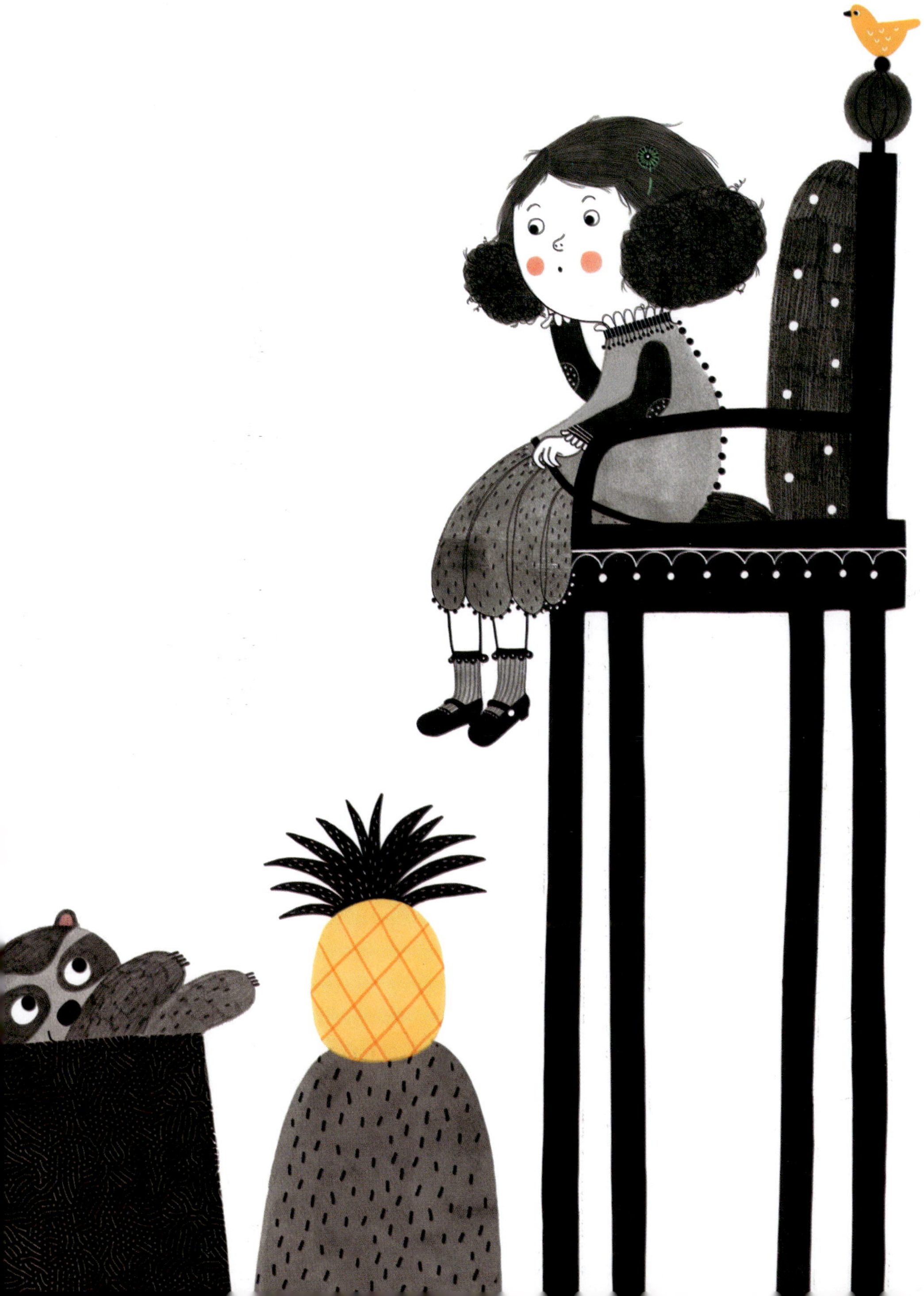

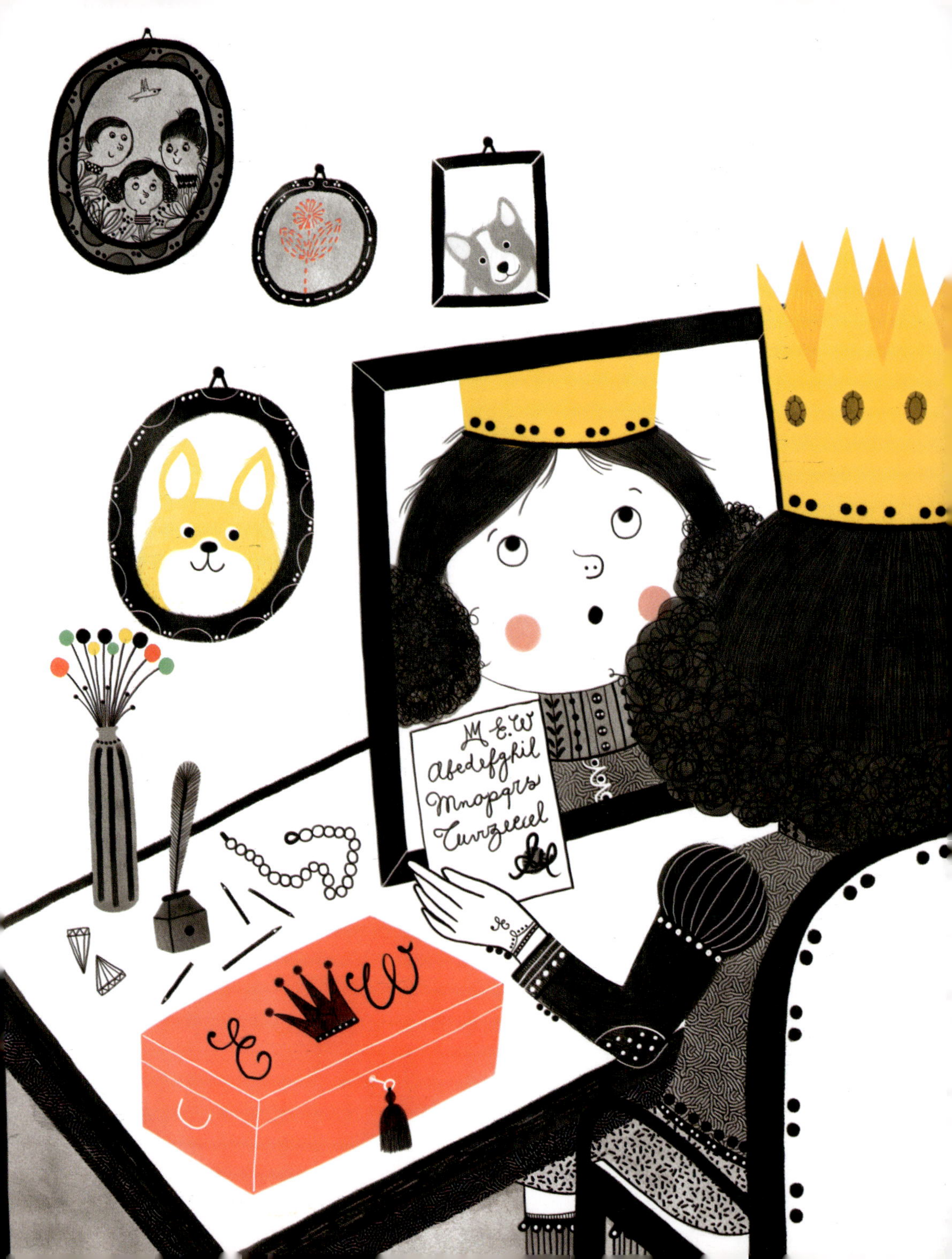

Soon, I will have to start learning how to be a queen—to curtsey, wear uniforms, and drink a lot of tea! How boring!

There is however one big advantage to being queen...

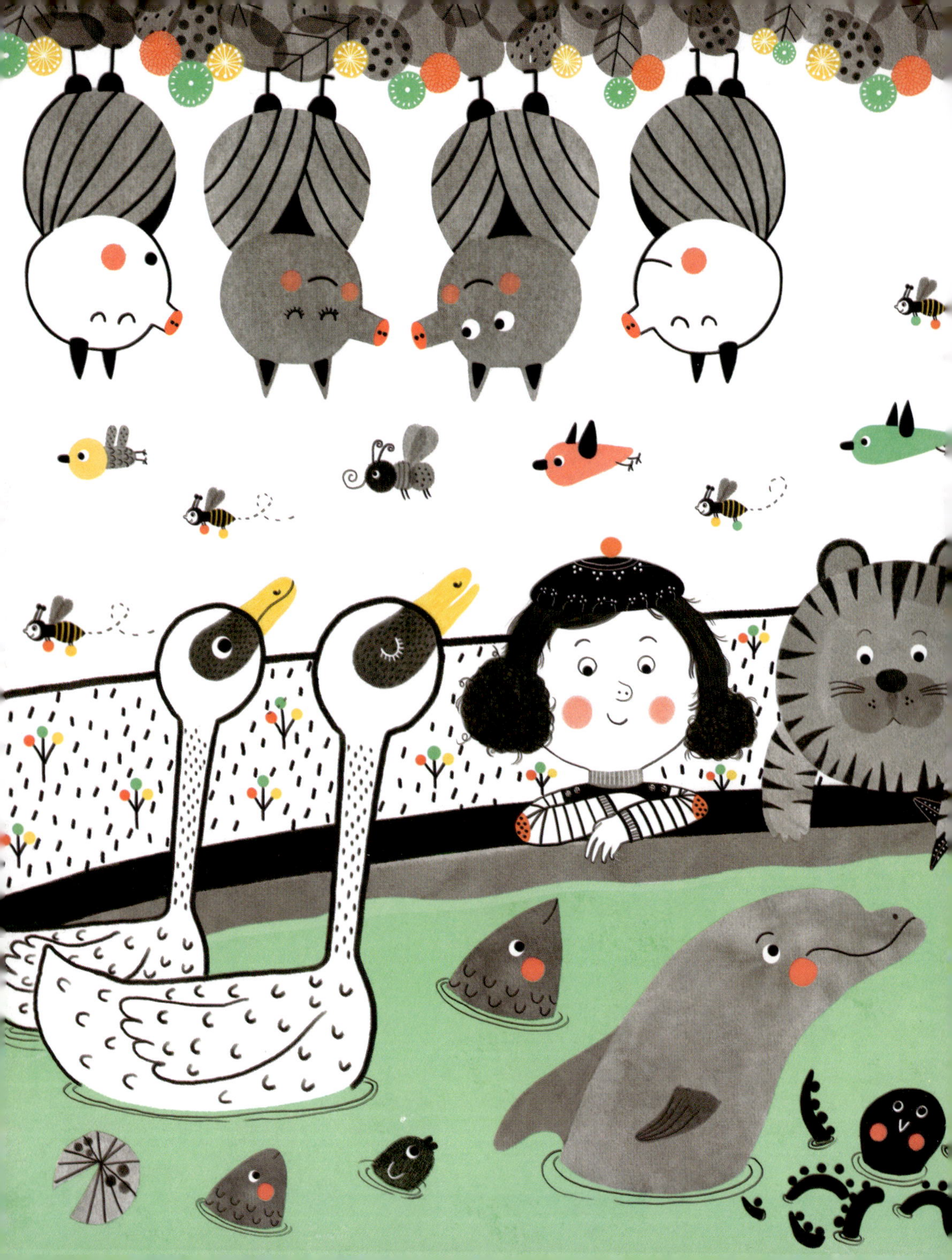

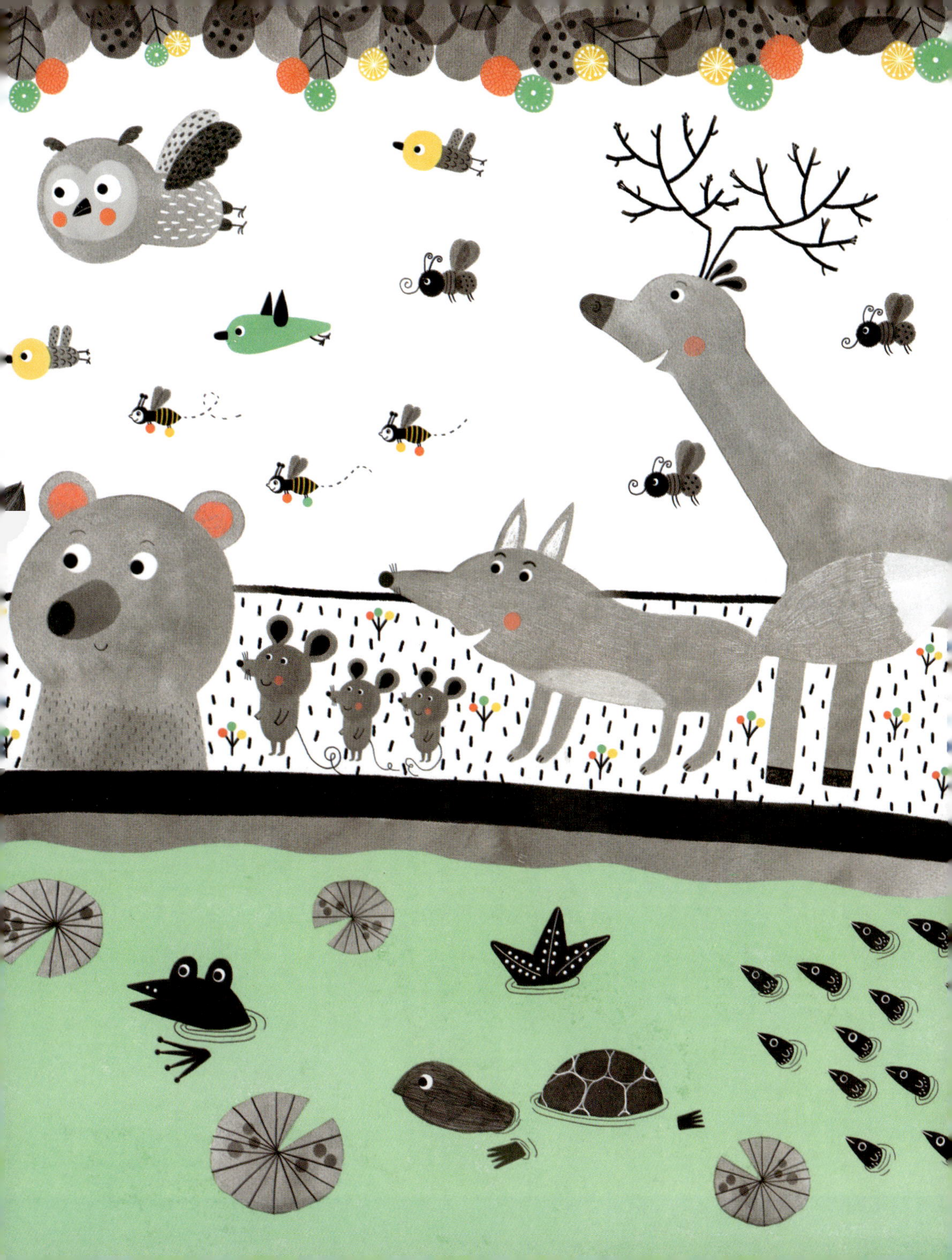

... I will be able to play
with all the animals in the kingdom!

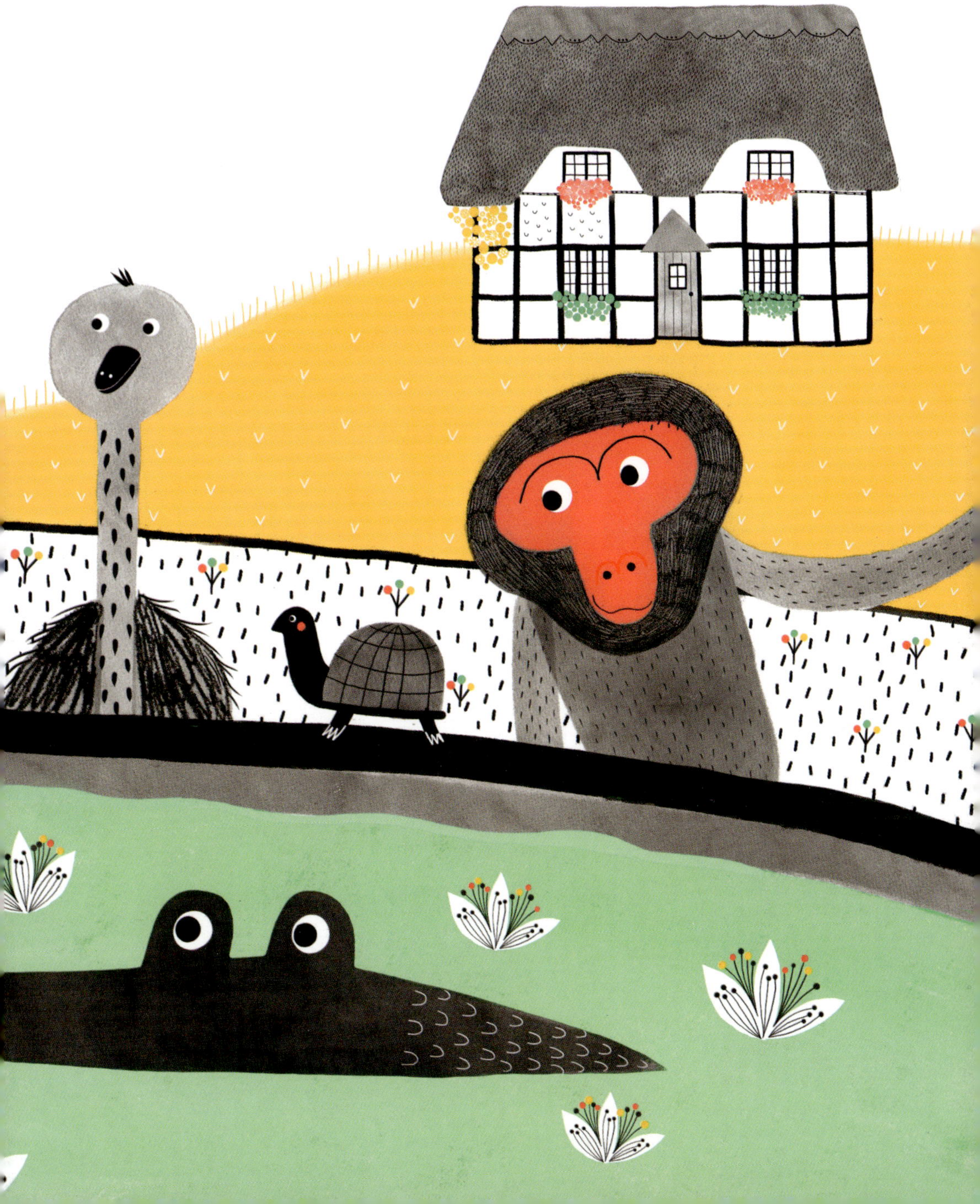

Maddalena Schiavo

After graduating with a degree in philosophy, Schiavo worked for years in a public library. Her passion for writing grew, together with that for reading, until she started writing for children. For some years, she has published picture books and children's books in Italy. Her books have received mention in the most important specialist magazines, including *Andersen* magazine, and in the national press. She also takes part in animated readings and workshops in schools, libraries, and bookstores.

Valeria Valenza

For years, Valenza has worked in illustrations for children and young readers, toy design, and the creation of educational imaging workshops for both children and adults. Today, she collaborates with a wide variety of publishing houses throughout Italy, the United Kingdom, the United States, and France.

WSKids — WHITE STAR KIDS

White Star Kids® is a registered trademark property of White Star s.r.l.

© 2022 White Star s.r.l.
Piazzale Luigi Cadorna, 6 - 20123 Milan, Italy
www.whitestar.it

Translation: TperTradurre S.r.l., Rome
Editing: Michele Suchomel-Casey

All rights reserved. No part of this publication may be reproduced, stored or transmitted in any form or by any means without written permission from the publisher.

First printing, December 2022

ISBN 978-88-544-1975-9
1 2 3 4 5 6   26 25 24 23 22

Printed and manufactured in Serbia by Grafostil

MIX
Paper from responsible sources
FSC® C178000

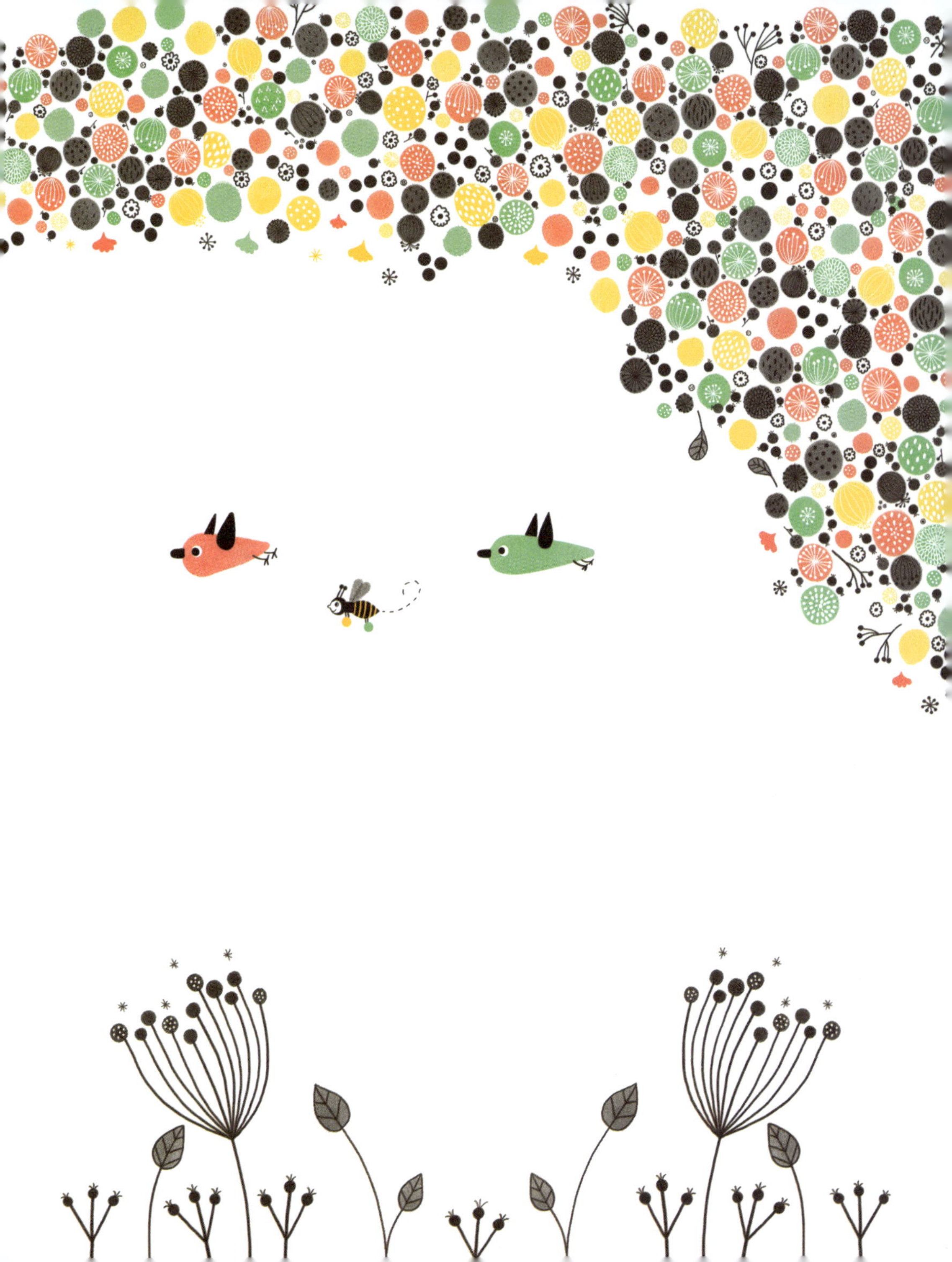